50 Water Dreams

CLEVELAND STATE UNIVERSITY POETRY CENTER
NEW POETRY

Caryl Pagel, Series Editor

Michael Dumanis, Founding Series Editor

For a complete listing of titles please visit www.csupoetrycenter.com

50 Water Dreams

Siwar Masannat

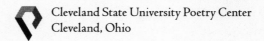
Cleveland State University Poetry Center
Cleveland, Ohio

ISBN 978-0-9860257-9-2

First edition

19   18   17   16   15   5   4   3   2   1

This book is published by the Cleveland State University Poetry Center,
2121 Euclid Avenue, Cleveland, Ohio 44115-2214
www.csupoetrycenter.com and is distributed by
SPD / Small Press Distribution, Inc. www.spdbooks.org.

Cover image: Nidal El-Khairy
50 Water Dreams was designed and typeset by Amy Freels in Centaur with Effloresce display.

LIBRARY OF CONGRESS CATALOGING-IN-PUBLICATION DATA
Masannat, Siwar.
  [Poems. Selections]
  50 water dreams / by Siwar Masannat. — First edition.
     pages cm — (New poets)
  ISBN 978-0-9860257-9-2 (alk. paper)
  I. Title. II. Title: Fifty water dreams.

PS3613.A7927A6 2015
811'.6—dc23

                              2015003488

For my family
Ayman, Roula, & Bassel

Contents

Let's pretend you 'had' a land. Then you 'lost' it. Now fondly describe it. That is pastoral.

Daughter of a Woman

Fadia is & her father is martyr. She is
on a mountain, radiant, unknown.
Says, *There will be no setting up tent:*
this light enough resting place.

       She prophesizes wind for fifty days.

When long ago she built the perfect home of lights &
stars to navigate, came envy. What if Ishmael never found
way to her home?

       Or, another desert of no lemon & orange orchard.
       One clementine the size of small fists.

Fadia says, *In a backyard of tomatoes. No horses or goats here,*
Father left them by the house.

I squat by sand, tell of Fadia's father, martyr.

Out from between two crouching masses of the world the word leapt

Ishmael is two men sometimes. His
mother's name in Arabic goes for immigrated

masculine. She was not masculine, to remember her
truly. She was treated, had heavy work, even

struck. Or maybe her deeds were as incense beautiful.
Here is her recompense: from hand to lap

to desert in a water puddle she found. Ishmael
has been called many things—to be redeemed

or be carnal & natural, a mere exile. Ishmael
is two of many, significant.

A Baptism: Water!

The lowest point on earth, on the sand
Fadia bends—

Ishmael leans toward her midriff,
slathering black onto olive skin. Fadia floats—

In his hands, her ponytail cannot
defy the pull toward sand.
"The Dead Sea cannot sustain romance,"

Ishmael says, "cells trafficking water out—
We are running out of water."

Air saturated between her nostrils
& his shoulder's coarse hairs.

On Origins of Ishmael

Identification of Hagar with the Jews ... was as old as Christianity itself;

> Hagar called Egyptian, Jewess, Muslim.
> Hagar suffering deserts, ones
> *already explained.*

Ishmael may not have one—a religion, that is.

> For example, who could approve Hagar's affliction?

However, Fadia always assumed he had *one; & that one.*

> Air in Arabic is *one stiff dick*—

I will proclaim Hagar contested-Egyptian-slave-Jewess-princess.

> *There are, perhaps, feelings: inimical*—

"Not for anybody this shade"

Ishmael when he knows, knows. *No,*
says Fadia, *as if he dragged the mare*
to water & she kicked him. I had thought

a scene not like this, rather:
sand in his eyes—
Hip along knee, animal unsaddled; Ishmael

settled down beneath a shade.

Talking over skin

Not a particular scent in the room,
rather the way glass windows reflect a face & his mother
walking in—a hint of a limp.

Rhythmic mouthing of words, a faster grip:
the way glasses fog up when breathed on—obstructing
clarity & eyes.

His mother's hip on the arm of a chair—an internal pleading.
Three once went to a living room & startled
each other with a memory each.

Handcuffed & blindfolded to stop them from trying to flee

His blue blender is whirring. What if

Fadia's finger slips in between blades?
Like citrus mist splashing eyes?

Ishmael measures the distance between

bed & wall & allocates it to Fadia.
Ishmael says Fadia likes tight areas,

so she may fill up space.

ACT: On Origins of Horse

Fadia: *Father left you by the iron gate—*

Horse: Before, though, I was with a wind-spout;
                whirled toward Ishmael.

Fadia: *How you galloped into the inner courtyard—*

Horse: Once, I stopped scattering dust and rain,
                & so gathered myself into prancing—
                I swallowed up the ground.

Ishmael: "archaeological evidence of
                a distinctive head shape;
                horses resemble modern Arabians;"

Fadia: *Horses resemble Arabs or Horse?*

Ishmael: "High tail carriage;
                Bloodlines date to centuries;"

Horse: Are not Arabian horses Semitic too?

Fadia, your back onto these olive walls

Then, to think twelve followed you:
you appeared woman,
between thighs—
such a feminine surprise.

When you had to you knew
to paint walls of your own
skin color. A meld in.

Ishmael couldn't tell you from concrete.
One day, he said, "Fadia,
your house is mine is how
it has always been written."

ACT: Confessional

I: Fadia, I wish I could say
                I saw nobody coming, so I went instead

Fadia: *I offer you my handkerchief:*
                All black irises I found embroidered

Ishmael: "spread-eagled, by my knee——"
                "Or maybe her knees came together. Eventually——"

Fadia: *A style not uncommon, in nature & geometry——*
                If I can, I will not let Ishmael throw unto you a stone——

Tales of a scorched earth

Ishmael if he dies
will his mother's tears
shame him?

Daughters were offered:
virgins instead of angels.

The angels, they were guests.
Who wear fire & sulphur.

Fadia, have you heard?
The warning by angels.

Have you heard? You have been called
"invented". There are skeptics.

Cities could have been Arabic for
fasten & fortify, deep & copious;
or Hebrew for scorched, a ruined heap.

Pastoral Interview

Why stoop to kiss this doorstep?

When land brought to pause disregard
the scriptural view of earth. It is fallacious.

This wind here not intruding on earth surface.

Ishmael is only a man from away.

Fadia, are you too woman, small & significant?

No goat-hair tent here but house of brick & concrete.

This house not of guns, but of you.

ACT of Expulsion

Fadia: *How Horse stays by the house—*

Horse: Once, I was created from southern winds.

Fadia: *This land: the smell of cardamom & hay*
                        between my father & Horse.

Horse: I was brought inside for shelter.

Horse keeping the house company; Horse humanizes the house; Horse socializes the house, or with the house.

Ishmael: "I am no guest, this house is mine
                        is how it has always been"

Fadia: *been scriptured?*

                        Horse is four thousand five hundred years old, of naturally good
                        disposition—proud, does not tolerate ineptitude or abuse.

Ishmael: "This house is mine is how it has always been"

Horse nuzzling a jasmine arc across the iron gate; Horse is near-divine, near a well, near walls not tent; Horse may keep the house from dying.

The mind of the Oriental, on the other hand, like his picturesque streets, is eminently wanting in symmetry. His reasoning is of the most slipshod description.

—Lord Cromer

Fadia responds to Cromer:

I feel the grit between my canines melt like ice with salt on it.

When they saw the trees did they know they would love the desert just
the same. An expanse laid out, hills, not plains of green, not plain—no planes
hovering in between layers of sky. Even planes never flew that high.

Green or desert demystified. Did they know of the water underneath?
Are we they, propped up against green grass looking up at pines?

Do blue & brown eyes mix to green & gray?

Our assonance: finding teeth caked in the soil of land, tongue dressed in sand—
no common vowels between long a's & o's & u's.

You look like you have just encountered a speck of dust in this breeze.

Ishmael classifies body shapes using English letters of the alphabet

A woman, a *p*, walking along a pier—her mother, a *c*, had once been a *p*. Bones can be malleable.

Ishmael's measure is depth of skin color, not hue

1.

"Fadia, say you have
skin, does it taste black?
Pickle with zest of lemon
I have plucked from your father's tree?"

2.

The romance here is this: Fadia's father is martyr & Ishmael's mother exile.

3.

What Ishmael does to uncover skin?
Today Fadia's olive, left in the sun,

does she turn from green to black?
Hue of cells scraped fleshy
white—or does it?

Fadia, let me scrub your arms, maybe Ishmael will
mistake them for his. Fadia, are you too woman
& alone in your father's house?

4.

Fadia says,   *My father was once*
crucified. They pulled me out of him,
baby bloody, full head of black
hair. My teeth they pried with crowbars.
I heard crows then, instead of River Jordan
running.

An evening once olives pickled
for dinner. Bread bubbling hot
& round. Then wine & clementines.
Bread dipped in olive oil & thyme.

5.

    "If you walk across the Red Sea do you hear
Pharaohs drowning—their salty deaths?"

ACT: Renouncing "p"

Alphabet Women:

Foreign letter—
Not in Arabic or geometry

"p":

To be named so, yet
shaped of bones not ribs

Fadia:

*If I can I will not let them throw
unto you a stone*

Oriental's Petra Verse

Ishmael: "Weather-torn & shorn mountain
                     Goat-hair tent beneath—
                     Legs crossed on desert sand"

Fadia: *from between two crouching rocks a rose door*

Ishmael: "a lapping tongue across—"

Fadia: *not licking, but latched door*

Ishmael: "a city once defeated by water—"

Fadia: *Siq, or shaft, dramatically naturally positioned—holding water.*

                  A cluster of dust sailing across to Wadi Mussa

On Fadia's Origins

Fadia, your father was a dead man forced to go home on foot:

martyr, he was. Unlike you; you ascended home, or was it not

home you ascended to? Doubly miraculous, it is. Both of you

martyrs of this land. *The desert will be covered with concrete*

springs sequestered by angels carrying blue swords.

Or not angels. Not swords, either. Rather, ground, space,

sea arms. I can see your arms, Fadia: & all you are is fingers.

Remember, how the English crucified your father

on a cactus tree?   His branches brittle like bones.

Dreams of Flight

Over the shack:
a rifle. & a man in it—
Border between sand & land.

Fadia picks bananas, oranges, tomatoes,
squeezes them back into ground.

ACT: Underlife

Alphabet Women: Under the bridge, under the bus
                   we carry beautiful eyes

Fadia: *How an olive tree is skinny——in its branches*

Alphabet Women: Do not lay down for a gaze, no veil & unveil:
                   we reveal red sand under fingernails

Fadia: *Our fingernails immersed*

Alphabet Women: Chase Ishmael away, chase sand from his eyes
                   so he shall see the olive tree & let her——

Fadia: *After the English crucified fathers on a cactus tree for*
                   two days & fathers never confessed

Alphabet Women: Then yesterday breaks——on the ground

Fadia: *Shrapnel of yesterday Ishmael constructs into a mirror:*
                   image not ours after us

Lots of guns...

Of my eye

Fadia, I say I dare not blink. If I could
hide you in my eyelids & the nation,

too. Skip the pencilling of that plane—

It can claim a rain after cautionary papers
have planted themselves by your pillow.

No—missiles signed—goat-hair
tent here—camp of concrete.

ACT of Fight & Flight

Fadia: *To judge by side of river or sea.*
                     Are all Semites transcendent?

I: The whiteness of Phosphorus against your olive—

Fadia: *In bones, not skin*

I: I have found framed by rectangles & glowing—

The women, their legs, where the air

Imposed, not exactly like Ishmael's settlement.
More as air & space arms reaching soil—

two different kinds of sour.
When land was branded with birth-

right; Fadia feels margins flow over—
knows them once there. Fadia eye-lit, tagged

& gagged under the bridge with dark green olive
leaves: a prickly-kind-of-taste this is—

feels pickled then jarred—

ACT: paste of blue cloud untangled itself on the red sky

(Fadia pulls on thread, unravelling it into heaps of blue)

Fadia: *for fifty days*
                    sand occupies wind
                    wind occupies air

(Fadia's limbs slide across. Fadia, widespread——)

Ishmael: "my red earth slid into air"

(The way the weight of Ishmael's chest hair on her back——)

Fadia: *a blood-stint in the distant sky*

(Ishmael holding Fadia by the feet)

Operation

Ishmael casts Fadia in lead—
a statue unlike organic,
not salt for looking back
but chiselled as after burning

For Light, or

Ishmael white—as
Phosphorus—to illuminate
Fadia, or her house,
bury flame in her bones

ACT: O Sharp & Smooth

Fadia (squints through a hole of a button)

Ishmael (chisels bone, shreds black, scatters)

Fadia (collects back by bolts & nails)

Ishmael (escalation)

Fadia (hears it):   *a mass drops across & among—straight through*

Fadia found at Dead Sea: O Sea Breeze

Not dead at sea but by
lake—biblical
setting, sitting, Fadia
peeling rind off fruit to eat—
or Fadia building sand
walls on the beach—

ACT: in a discrete series the last abstract entry dropped

Fadia (looking)

Ishmael (watching water from ceiling fall in plops)

Fadia (hears it):   *a skull can take only so much water*

Ishmael (knee deep in a tissue mass benign)

ACT: Occupation

Ishmael: "These faraway tents are!

       You build them in multiplicity & again..."

Fadia: *I was once asked if "imposed" is essentially bad—*
       I said: implanting settlements is

Ishmael: "Both not distant—

(Rather, Fadia should have inherited her own, occupied land)

I just want to be held, but contingently, the way the mind holds
a trauma ~~that failed to take place.~~

Fadia dreams her dream comes in glass

Fadia blows on sand, hot
to transparency or scalding
is grain melting—Fadia not
melding & what it is to be
sand to glass

Fadia sculpting into transparency

Fadia thinks to bring eye closer
to nudge—smaller this distance
to mouth not to pull but touch
as seen before thought becomes
now not unsaid

On Passivity

When the pronoun prohibited is,
Fadia & I take down partitions:

each she pulls to periphery a side of curtain.
How Ishmael is left standing feet over

wounds. A city. Or, a city with wounds.
A performance we undramatized.

ACTS: Fucking is a house falling down

I: Fadia's doorstep is hers

Fadia: *And the windowsill, too.*
                I could invite you in, Ishmael,

I: But if she chooses not to then away
                like a flower sends meadows to other towns...

Fadia: *Out of this gate, Ishmael, go.*

On Diglossia

I speak such as her.

Verbs gendered, god
an expression secular

in expression always,

a house masculine, the
nation feminine.

Where my mouth grazes
the corner of Fadia's lip.

Fadia,

These consonants are slippery.
Is it *Dabkeh* you said?—

a thousand birds for one morning,
chirping? Laundry
lines as they should

droop with your stone-filled
pant pockets.

Song for eyes

1.

What is it that averted
my eyes off yours, Fadia—
or is the word Arabic, a word for reply?

My eyes—eyelids heavy— is it
sleep? Between your eyes & mine
a rifle.

2.

Fucking—is it anger in the hazel
of your eyes? Might be
the perpetual green of your land.
I will blow on olive
trees until the fake branches

disappear, or pluck black
irises for a wedding wreath.

3.

Fadia, please come flying
over pillars, all seven of them
& the wisdom will rub me until
I come flying too—I warn you: I may be eating
my words behind the hem
of your skirt.　　　On the hill,

rather your courtyard,
Ishmael built himself a dwelling.

4.

Come for words under the desert, not Ishmael's
fists under searching
for kin he killed by friendly fire.

I have seen them all, framed by black rectangles & glowing.
Their eyes nothing in them hazel.

5.

What is more beautiful than a coffee cup:
Arabic, or cardamom flakes arranging
your fortune   I see
horses in your cup,

saucer tells of a leaving:
is it hay around your wrists,
or tattooed, a bracelet gold?

A line of poetry is house to intend a poem

To wake up to yellow pollen on the balcony
not sprinkled red sand on a chair outside.

Lawn on the ground naturally
trimmed—rolling around in it I skin

my knee, green blades running into
it sharp—Fadia asks, *do you unroll your r's?*

Implications of Martyrdom

Fadia, I see you have a piece
of luck: died, more than once
you had that skin flayed off of you.

You say, *fuck you, am*
not the land fertile not the land holy—

All I do is see you go back
to stone & concrete shed & wall.
You do not see. I am not

looking to see this grove
or orchard or Dead
Sea turn sulphurous underneath

these fingernails.

Pastoral Interview

What is causality,
for x to lead to y? What
is loss of land?

A morning dew, then
dismantled home to house
to tent. A process

am not privy to.
What is it that works?
An olive orchard, grapes, lots

of tomatoes, grown to taste.
How do you move with both arms
broken, fingernails pulled?

I walk.

Visions of a home return

Let Alphabet women
see their reflections,
how posture regained

itself straight & their arms
unclasped on their chests or by
the chests or over their breasts.

They are all eyes & all I see, Fadia.
Arms extended & hands
reaching out for rain.

The reins on Horse
will be replaced.

Someday, Fadia, as you & I going back—

A Drunken Serenade

I want to put you in my revolution,
Fadia said; arak swirling
in flasks unlouched—the liquorice,

the aniseed—*I want you*
with eyes so dark alleys look
lit. With hair so thick

it is strand by strand
the million birds—now doves—
diving nose to feet.

A bullet in the desert is not unnatural

Neither is woman on Fadia's body
every day tenderly & night & in these ways
forbidden, unlike bullets. I say,

I understand you will not leave
Horse alone in the house, rather stay
regardless cautionary papers raining down

sky plentiful. Our desert not red every day, it does
grow irises & irrigate towns when dug down.
You say, *Ishmael might take bullets unlost in sand*

finding his blue tanks' way away——

Poetry is not adornment, a truth

I don't see how you, pried
open for all the world to see—

How I would like an argument
with you to go to the soil & make it

grow grapes. Of my mouth
nothing fell out as it might
or ought—*You make*
wine I make water to tell
Ishmael it is so & as such.

That it is not us.
Such is a trope.

A time we plant one black
iris on the windowsill:
we watch it—

Why did you leave Horse alone?

This world, horses keeping
houses, is not how we always
return. & I, Fadia, will not leave

till air decides to drop this dirt
into place. This world, not ours,
is what is told. I would hold

an olive tree, shake it, till
its fruit falls; you hold the
children & once at last

tell them: their just stones.
How is this if not to sing?
Who has been known

to mourn will do. In my hand,
three olives squeezed into
oil for your forehead,

not to anoint—& I hear
horses coming along.

Notes

This book is in conversation with Mahmoud Darwich and Marcel Khalifeh. There are loose translations of pieces of poems and songs throughout the manuscript.

The book epigraph is from Lisa Robertson's *XEclogue*. The title "Out from Between..." is from Anne Carson's *Autobiography of Red*. The epigraph to "On Origins of Ishmael" is from *Jewish Expulsion and Jewish Exile in Scholastic Thought* by Deeana Copeland Klepper. *already explained* is from Zaid Shlah. "Not for Anybody This Shade" borrows a translated title from Ziad Rahbani. "Tales of a scorched earth" is a Smashing Pumpkins song title, and "invented" in the poem refers to Newt Gingrich's comment on Palestinian people. "Why stoop to kiss this doorstep?" is from Anne Carson's *Autobiography of Red*. The epigraph to "Fadia Responds to Cromer:" is from Edward Said's *Orientalism*. "On Fadia's Origins..." borrows language from Etel Adnan. "Lots of guns" is borrowed from Anne Carson's *Decreation*. The O's refer to Israeli military operations: the war on Gaza in 2008–09 (Operation Cast Lead), the Baalbek operation during the war on Lebanon (Operation Sharp & Smooth), and the Gaza Flotilla Raid (Operation Sea Breeze). "the women, their legs, where the air" is borrowed from Rosmarie Waldrop's *Love, Like Pronouns*. "A line of poetry is house to intend a poem" is a translation of a Tarek Abu Kwaik lyric. The epigraph to section (3) is from Ben Lerner's *Angle of Yaw*. "Fucking is a house falling down" is from *Jane Sexes it Up: true confessions of feminist desire*. Many poems borrow language from John Berryman's *The Dream Songs*.

Acknowledgments

I am indebted to Daniel D'Angelo, Alyse Knorr, Katherine Swett, and Peter Twal for their invaluable friendship and support, as well as for looking at various drafts of these poems and offering feedback. To my family and friends in Jordan and the US, thank you for your loving presence.

My gratitude to the George Mason M.F.A. community for their generous support and mentorship: Amal Amireh, Jennifer Atkinson, Sally Keith, Bill Miller, Eric Pankey, and especially, Susan Tichy. My thanks to all my classmates, for their friendship and community, and especially to Brian Fitzpatrick, Bryan Koen, Rachel Graham, M. Mack, Sarah Marcus, Jack Snyder, Kate Partridge, Mike Walsh, and Susan Whalen.

Thanks to the editors of the following journals, in which some of these poems appeared, sometimes in earlier versions: *APARTMENT*: "Oriental's Petra Verse", "Of my eye", "ACT: Underlife", "Song for eyes"; *VOLT*: "Pastoral Interview" and "Pastoral Interview"; *New Orleans Review* : "Fadia Responds to Cromer", "A line of poetry is house to intend a poem", "Why did you leave the horse alone?", "A bullet in the desert is not unnatural", "Poetry is not adornment, a truth"; *B O D Y*: "The Daughter of Woman", "Out from between two crouching masses of the world the word leapt", "On Fadia's Origins" and "On Origins of Ishmael"; and *Eleven Eleven*: "A Baptism: Water!"

My deep gratitude to everyone at CSU Poetry Center and to Ilya Kaminsky for selecting the book.

About the Author

Siwar Masannat is an Arab writer from Amman, Jordan. She holds an M.F.A. in poetry from George Mason University and is currently pursuing a Ph.D. in Creative Writing at the University of Wisconsin-Milwaukee. Siwar co-founded *Gazing Grain Press*, a chapbook publisher open to feminists of every gender and sexuality. Her poems and articles have appeared in *Denver Quarterly*, *VOLT*, *Gargoyle*, and *7iber.me*, among others.